How to Draw the Life and Times of

Dwight D. Eisenhower

Ryan P. Randolph

The Rosen Publishing Group's
PowerKids Press™
New York

To my father, William Randolph

Published in 2006 by The Rosen Publishing Group, Inc.
29 East 21st Street, New York, NY 10010

First Edition

Editor: Daryl Heller
Layout Design: Albert Hanner, Greg Tucker
Photo Researcher: Amy Feinberg

Illustration Credits: All illustrations by Elana Davidian.
Photo Credits: pp. 4, 12 (bottom), 26 (top) © Corbis; p. 7 © Hank Walker/Time Life Pictures/Getty
Images; p. 8 Presidential Avenue/G. Zuck; p. 9 Gary Sewell/Herald-Democrat; p. 10 Eisenhower
Presidential Library; p. 12 (top) © David J. & Janice L. Frent Collection/Corbis; p. 14 National Archives;
p. 16 (top) © Moore/Keystone/Getty Images, (bottom) © Hulton-Deutsch Collection/Corbis; p. 20 ©
maps.com/Corbis; p. 22 Library of Congress Prints and Photographs Division; p. 24 © Bettmann/Corbis;
p. 28 White House Historical Association (White House Collection).

Library of Congress Cataloging-in-Publication Data

Randolph, Ryan P.
How to draw the life and times of Dwight D. Eisenhower / Ryan P. Randolph.
p. cm. — (A kid's guide to drawing the presidents of the United States of America) Includes index.
ISBN 1-4042-3010-6 (library binding)
1. Eisenhower, Dwight D. (Dwight David), 1890–1969—Juvenile literature. 2. Presidents—United
States—Biography—Juvenile literature. 3. Drawing—Technique—Juvenile literature. I. Title. II. Series.
E836.R35 2006
973.921'092—dc22

2005013781

Printed in China

Contents

Meet Dwight David Eisenhower

From 1953 until 1961, Dwight David Eisenhower served two four-year terms as the thirty-fourth president of the United States. Eisenhower had risen to fame as a U.S. general in World War II.

World War II was a global conflict that was fought from 1939 until 1945. In this war Great Britain, France, the Soviet Union, the United States, China, and the other Allies battled Germany, Italy, and Japan.

Eisenhower planned the 1944 D-Day invasion, or attack, of France, which was then under the control of Nazi Germany. On D-Day, which was June 6, about 156,000 Allied soldiers landed on the beaches of Normandy, France. This mass attack would finally lead to the defeat of Nazi Germany.

After World War II, Eisenhower's popularity with the American people was quite high. Later he was easily elected president for two terms. As both a general and a president, Eisenhower was a strong leader. He was intelligent, fair, and able to make hard decisions.

President Eisenhower often proclaimed to Americans that he was not a politician, he was just a simple soldier.

Dwight D. Eisenhower was born in Denison, Texas, in 1890, but spent most of his childhood in Abilene, Kansas. Young Eisenhower did well in school. However, his favorite activity as a boy was playing sports, especially football.

In 1911, at the age of 21, Eisenhower entered the United States Military Academy at West Point. Upon his graduation in 1915, he began his long career as a soldier in the U.S. Army.

You will need the following supplies to draw the life and times of Dwight D. Eisenhower:

✓ A sketch pad   ✓ An eraser   ✓ A pencil   ✓ A ruler

These are some of the shapes and drawing terms you need to know:

Horizontal Line	——	Squiggly Line	⌇
Oval	⬭	Trapezoid	⏢
Rectangle	▭	Triangle	△
Shading	▰	Vertical Line	|
Slanted Line	/	Wavy Line	∿

The Presidency of Dwight D. Eisenhower

In 1952, Dwight D. Eisenhower ran as the Republican candidate for president. "I Like Ike" was the campaign slogan, or saying. That slogan was both successful and true. Eisenhower is rated as one of the most popular U.S. presidents of the twentieth century. Eisenhower easily defeated his Democratic competitor Adlai Stevenson twice, first in the election of 1952, and then again in 1956.

Eisenhower was president during a period of peace and economic success in America. The bloodshed of World War II was over. Americans were simply glad to be alive and safe in their homes. Eisenhower's biggest challenge as president was the cold war.

During the cold war, relations between the United States and the Soviet Union, a Communist country, were hostile. Both sides feared each other, especially since both sides had nuclear weapons. Although the two sides did not fight each other directly, their relationship was strained. Eisenhower worked hard to keep peace and protect the United States.

This photograph of President Dwight D. Eisenhower was taken in June 1960, in Alaska. President Eisenhower was a member of the Republican Party, which is one of the two largest U.S. political parties. The other major political party is the Democratic Party.

Eisenhower's Texas

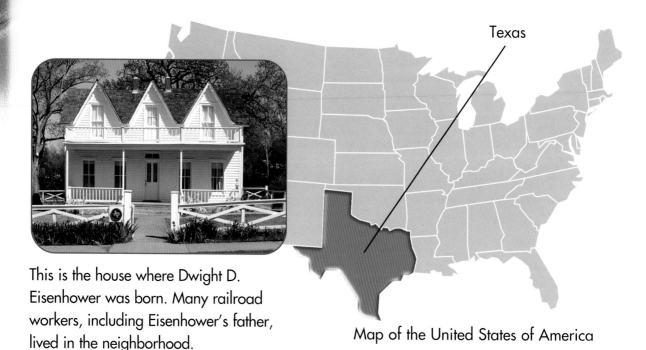

This is the house where Dwight D. Eisenhower was born. Many railroad workers, including Eisenhower's father, lived in the neighborhood.

Texas

Map of the United States of America

Dwight D. Eisenhower was born in Denison, Texas, in 1890, to David and Ida Eisenhower. Dwight was the third of seven sons. Eisenhower's father had moved to Denison in 1888 because it was the only place he could find work on the railroads.

In 1889, Ida moved from her home in Kansas to Texas to join her husband in a small two-story house by the railroad tracks. Dwight Eisenhower was the only child in his family to be born in Denison. The family moved to Abilene, Kansas, in 1892, when Dwight Eisenhower was just two years old.

The house where Eisenhower was born is now a Texas state historic site. A site is the place where a historic event occurred. The site, which is called the Eisenhower Birthplace State Park, has a visitor's center and an education building where people can learn more about Eisenhower. Later in his life, Eisenhower began painting pictures. The visitor's center has two of his paintings on exhibit.

Denison also honored Eisenhower by naming the Eisenhower State Park after him. The park is on Lake Texoma. Visitors to the park can go hiking, biking, and swimming. They can also observe the region's wildlife.

This bronze statue of Dwight D. Eisenhower was unveiled at the Eisenhower Birthplace State Park in 1973. Robert Lee Dean Jr., the sculptor, looked at nearly 1,000 pictures of Eisenhower before he selected a 1945 image of Eisenhower to use. Dean depicted General Eisenhower in his World War II army uniform. On federal holidays flags are placed around the statue.

A Military Career

Dwight D. Eisenhower entered the United States Military Academy at West Point in 1911. West Point is the college in New York State at which the U.S. Army trains young people to be officers, or leaders in the army. He graduated in 1915, and was stationed at Fort Sam Houston in San Antonio, Texas.

When the United States entered World War I in 1917, Eisenhower wanted to fight in Europe. However, he had proved himself such a good teacher of soldiers that he was sent instead to train soldiers on how to use a tank, the new wartime armored car shown above. Eisenhower was made the commander of Camp Colt in Gettysburg, Pennsylvania. Because all the new tanks were being used to fight the war in Europe, there were no real tanks available for training. Instead Eisenhower used trucks with machine guns on them to teach the soldiers. World War I ended in 1918 with a victory for the United States and its allies, France and Britain. After the war Eisenhower served as an aide, or assistant, to several experienced generals.

1 On the facing page, Eisenhower stands before a tank. To begin drawing the tank draw a large rectangular guide. Inside the guide add two smaller rectangles as shown. The top rectangle is smallest.

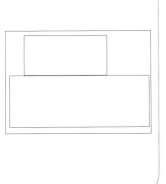

2 Inside the top rectangular guide, add three smaller rectangles as shown. Next draw two ovals. These ovals will be your guides for drawing the wheels. The oval on the right is slightly higher.

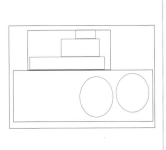

3 Add all the lines you see to the rectangles you added in step 2. Start from the top and add curved and slanted lines to each section. Take your time.

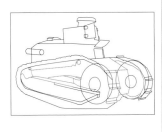

4 Erase extra lines. Draw the small shape on the top left. Add two small ovals inside the larger ovals. Use curved and slanted lines to draw the shape next to the left oval as shown.

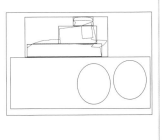

5 Add details along the top of the tank as shown. Using slanted lines add a window. Add curving and slanted lines, as well as both short and long lines around the tank's wheels.

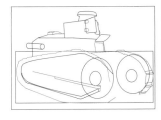

6 Erase the bottom rectangular guide from step 1. Add more details to the wheels as shown. Notice how the lines are added behind and between the two wheels.

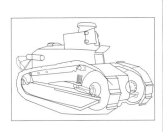

7 Draw the details at the back of the tank. Add lines and shapes to the wheels, too. Be sure to draw the small circles in the right wheel and inside the shape that extends from the left wheel.

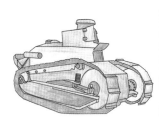

8 Erase the rectangular guide you made in step 1. Erase any extra lines. Finish your tank by shading.

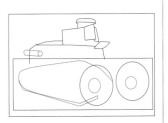

Mamie Eisenhower and Family

In 1915, shortly after Dwight D. Eisenhower had graduated from West Point, he met Mamie Geneva Doud in San Antonio, Texas. Mamie lived with her family in Denver, Colorado, but had come to Texas on vacation. The couple fell in love and were married in Denver on July 1, 1916. They had two sons together. Doud Dwight Eisenhower, shown with his parents in the bottom image, was born in 1917, but he died of scarlet fever in 1921. The couple's second son, John Sheldon Doud Eisenhower, was born in 1922.

The Eisenhowers moved from army base to army base during the 1920s and the 1930s. This included stays in Panama from 1922 to 1924, and the Philippines from 1935 to 1939. In Panama the military housing provided by the army for the Eisenhowers was small and always smelled of mildew. Despite the constant moving, the Eisenhowers were a happy family.

1

The top image on the facing page is a set of Mrs. Eisenhower and President Eisenhower shakers for salt and pepper. To begin drawing the Mamie Eisenhower shaker draw a large rectangle. Next add an oval and a smaller rectangle as shown.

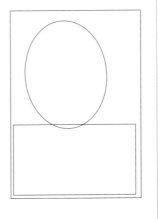

2

Using squiggly and curving lines, draw the outline of Mrs. Eisenhower's head, scarf, and the top of her body. Use the guide shapes you made in step 1 to help you. Notice how the body tips down slightly to the left.

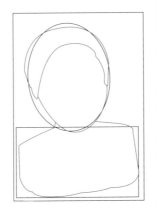

3

Erase the oval and rectangle you made in step 1. Add a squiggly line for the bangs at her forehead. Using curved lines draw the ribbon as shown. Add four straight lines that you will use as guides to draw her eyes, nose, and mouth.

4

Draw outlines around her eyes. Add her nose. Draw two curving lines to make her mouth. Add a curved line for the neckline of her dress as shown. Draw a small rough circle in the center of the neckline for a decorative flower.

5

Add two curved lines for eyebrows. Draw two small circles for the pupils of her eyes. Use squiggly lines to make armholes in her dress. Use two curving lines to make her necklace. Add a few lines to the flower on her dress. Add an earring on the left ear.

6

Erase the large rectangular guide you made in step 1. Erase the guides for the face you made in step 3. Finish your likeness of Mrs. Mamie Eisenhower by shading your drawing. Her hair, ribbon, dress, and flower are darker than the other areas.

World War II Begins

In 1939, Adolf Hitler's Nazi German army attacked Poland as part of Hitler's goal to conquer Europe. France and Britain then went to war with Germany. By 1940, many U.S. military leaders knew the United States had to prepare to fight Germany, Japan, and Italy.

On December 7, 1941, Japanese planes attacked a U.S. naval base at Pearl Harbor, Hawaii. The United States entered World War II shortly after. Dwight D. Eisenhower was sent to Washington, D.C., to work in the War Plans Division under General George Marshall, the head of the army. This division plotted how to fight the Germans and the Japanese. They also made sure that soldiers had supplies, weapons, and means of travel. By June 1942, Eisenhower had been made a general, and Marshall sent him to London to lead the U.S. forces in Europe. By the time Eisenhower took command, the Germans, who controlled most of Europe, had defeated France.

1

The U.S. Navy created the World War II poster on the facing page after the attack on Pearl Harbor. Begin creating the ship by drawing three rectangular guides as shown.

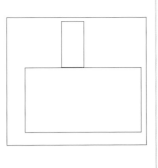

2

Inside the smallest rectangle, draw an oval and two slanted lines. Inside the larger rectangular guide draw two curving lines as shown.

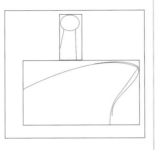

3

Inside the oval you made in step 2, draw the shapes shown. Add two more slanted lines beneath the oval. Add two rectangles as shown. Add an oval to the base of the ship.

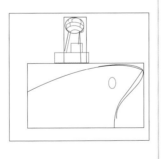

4

Erase the top rectangular guide from step 1 and the oval guide from step 2. Add shapes inside the two small rectangular guides. Connect the shapes to the curved lines you drew in step 2.

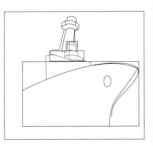

5

Erase extra lines. Add more lines to the top and midsection of the ship as shown. Start from the top and work your way down.

6

Add a number of shapes to the midsection of the ship. Add the two shapes to the small oval on the bottom section of the ship.

7

Erase any extra lines. Draw more shapes that extend from the side of the ship. Use squiggly lines to draw the waves around the ship.

8

Erase the large rectangular guide from step 1. Erase any extra lines where the waves overlap the lines of the ship. Finish your drawing by shading.

D-Day

In November 1942, General Eisenhower directed a successful Allied invasion of North Africa to push the Germans from the region. In the summer of 1943, the Allies attacked Sicily, Italy.

Eisenhower and the Allies then planned to push the Germans out of France. He and his staff organized a secret invasion in London, England. The Allied forces would proceed from the southern coast of England and land along the beaches of Normandy in northwest France. The first day of the attack required 156,000 men, who were to be moved on about 7,000 ships, including the special landing craft shown above. The name of the invasion was Operation Overlord. On June 6, 1944, Operation Overlord began. The day of the invasion was called D-Day. Many soldiers lost their lives on that day and in the coming months as Eisenhower led the Allied forces against the Germans. On May 8, 1945, the Germans officially surrendered, or gave up. The fighting in Europe was over.

1

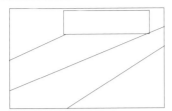

To start drawing a landing craft, which could be driven on land as well as sailed in the water, draw a large rectangular guide. Inside this rectangle draw a smaller rectangle and three slanted lines as shown.

2

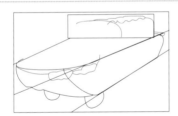

Using the three slanted lines as guides, draw several lines for the bottom half of the craft. Below these lines add two curved shapes for the wheels of the craft.

3

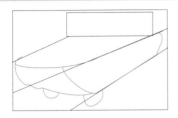

Use curved lines to add the rope that is tied to the craft. Add the two lumpy shapes connected to the rope. Use more squiggly and curving lines to begin drawing the top portion of the craft.

4

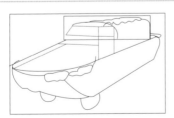

Erase the bottom two slanted lines you made in step 1. Then use straight and slanted lines to add windows and detail lines to the front and side of the craft.

5

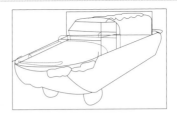

Draw a curved shape along the front of the craft as shown. Draw the shape that is along the front left side of the craft. Add the other lines to the top of the tank's front section.

6

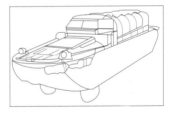

Erase the rectangular guide and the last slanted line you made in step 1. Add curved shapes for the two headlights. Add more shapes and lines to the window and to the front and the side of the tank as shown.

7

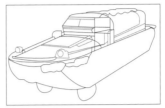

Erase any extra lines. Add curved and straight lines to the roof and to the side of the craft as shown. Using straight lines add details to the top of the craft's front. Add lines to the shapes connected to the ropes.

8

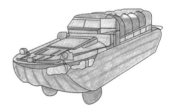

Erase the large rectangular guide you made in step 1. Erase any extra lines. Finish your craft by shading. On D-Day landing crafts were used to carry men and weapons from large military ships to the shore.

Life After the War

World War II officially ended after the Japanese surrendered in September 1945. Dwight D. Eisenhower returned to Washington, D.C. He took over as the army chief of staff, or head of the U.S. Army. In this post Eisenhower led the large demobilization, or the act of bringing soldiers home from Europe and Japan.

Eisenhower served for two years before resigning, or choosing to leave, the army in 1948. At 57 years old, Eisenhower took his first civilian job. He became president of Columbia University in New York City.

Eisenhower was not at Columbia for long, however. In 1950, Eisenhower was called to command the troops of the United States and of some western European nations in the North Atlantic Treaty Organization (NATO). NATO was the peacetime alliance, or partnership, of the United States, Britain, France, and other western European nations. NATO, whose sign is shown above, had been formed to protect western Europe from what many in the West thought was a possible military threat, or danger, from the Soviet Union in the East.

1

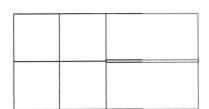

To begin drawing the NATO symbol, or sign, draw a large rectangle. Draw a vertical line in the center. To the left of this vertical line add another vertical line and a horizontal line as shown. To the right add a narrow horizontal rectangle as shown.

2

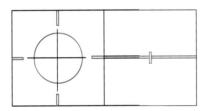

Add a circle on the left that crosses through the lines you made in step 1. Erase part of the lines that extend beyond the circle as shown. Add four small rectangles, as shown, on the left and one on the right. Erase the extra lines where the two rectangles intersect, or cross over each other, in the right square.

3

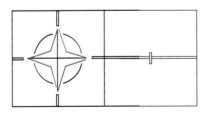

Erase the parts of the circle that cross through the lines. Using the crossing lines as your guide, add six slanted lines to create the shape of a star.

4

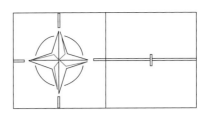

Add more slanted lines through the center of the star shape you made in step 3. Notice how these lines bend and make angles.

5

Add the outline for the word "NATO" inside the top right rectangle. Add the outline for the letters "OTAN," which is NATO spelled backward, inside the bottom right rectangle.

6

Thicken the curved lines around the star shape. Finish by shading. Leave the letters, parts of the star shape, and the lines under the letters white. Shade the rest of the drawing as shown. Notice which parts are colored before you begin.

The Korean War

Dwight D. Eisenhower was a national hero after the success of D-Day and his leadership in World War II. Both Democrats and Republicans wanted him to be a presidential candidate in 1952. Eisenhower ran as a Republican because he was conservative and shared many of the Republican Party's views. Eisenhower easily won the election of 1952 against the Democratic challenger Adlai Stevenson.

Just after he was elected, President Eisenhower flew to Asia to observe the ongoing conflict in Korea. Two years earlier on June 25, 1950, Communist forces from North Korea had attacked the democratic nation of South Korea. The United Nations army, which was led by the United States, defended South Korea. Communist China, however, soon aided North Korea. By 1952, both sides had fought to a bloody standstill. Eisenhower reviewed the United States' options and chose to stop fighting. In July 1953, North Korea, China, and the United Nations Command signed a formal agreement to end the war.

1

To begin drawing a map of North Korea and South Korea, draw a large rectangular guide. Then draw the shape shown using squiggly lines. These shapes will guide you as you draw the map.

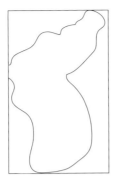

2

Use a squiggly line to draw the outline of North Korea as shown. Both North Korea and South Korea are in East Asia. These two nations are part of a peninsula, which is a large area of land that is nearly surrounded by water.

3

Use a squiggly line to draw the outline of South Korea as shown. The capital of North Korea is P'yongyang. The capital of South Korea is Seoul.

4

Add labels to your map. Label the top part of the map North Korea. Label the bottom half of your map South Korea.

5

Erase the guidelines around North Korea and South Korea that you made in step 1. Add a label for P'yongyang, the capital of North Korea. Add a label for Seoul, the capital of South Korea.

6

Erase the rectangular guide you made in step 1. Finish your map of North Korea and South Korea by shading the two nations. Shade North Korea darker than South Korea.

McCarthyism

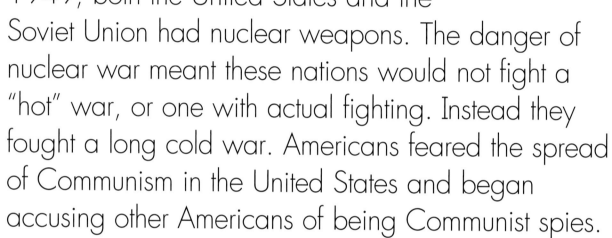

After World War II, the relationship between the United States, a democracy, and the Communist Soviet Union became worse. By 1949, both the United States and the Soviet Union had nuclear weapons. The danger of nuclear war meant these nations would not fight a "hot" war, or one with actual fighting. Instead they fought a long cold war. Americans feared the spread of Communism in the United States and began accusing other Americans of being Communist spies.

Joseph McCarthy, a Republican senator from Wisconsin, led the hunt for Communists. His attacks on accused Communists became known as McCarthyism. Senator McCarthy's attacks often violated constitutional freedoms, such as freedom of speech. Eisenhower refused either to condemn or to support McCarthy, even when McCarthy wrongly accused people. For this Eisenhower was faulted, as shown in the cartoon above. Finally, however, when McCarthy began questioning members of the U.S. Army, the Senate officially stopped McCarthy.

1 This 1953 cartoon shows Senator Joseph McCarthy (right) trying to control President Eisenhower. To begin drawing McCarthy draw a large rectangle. Add an oval and two lines as shown.

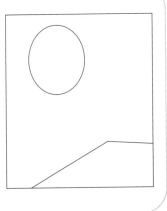

2 Inside the oval add a curved line to draw the shape of the head. Draw four straight lines as guides for the shoulders and arms. Draw four ovals to make guides for the hands and the feet as shown.

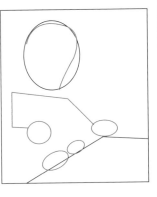

3 Add guides for the eye, mouth, jaw, and ear. On the left draw a curved line for the body. To make guides for the pen and ink, add two ovals and a straight line as shown.

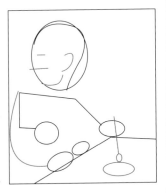

4 Using your guides draw the details of the eye, nose, mouth, and chin. Add squiggly and curving lines to draw the shape of McCarthy's arms, body, and legs.

5 Erase the oval, eye, and mouth guides. Draw the eyebrow and add details to the ear, nose, and face. Add lines for the jacket. Draw the hands and feet as shown. Notice how he is holding the pen.

6 Erase the arms, hands, and feet guides. Erase the lines where the feet overlap the desk. Draw the shirt and tie. Add lines to the shoes. Write "McCARTHY" on the leg on the left. Add lines to the pen and inkwell.

7 Erase the guides for the pen and inkwell. Draw the hair as shown. Draw small teardrop shapes for the splashing ink. Add the remaining lines to the inkwell.

8 Erase extra lines where the pen and hand overlap. Finish your drawing of McCarthy by shading. Shade his hair and eyebrows dark. Shade his suit, tie, part of his shoes, and the inkwell dark, too.

Ike and Civil Rights

America's economic success in the 1950s and Dwight D. Eisenhower's popularity led to his reelection in 1956. Soon after,

Eisenhower turned his attention to civil rights. In 1954, the U.S. Supreme Court's decision on *Brown v. Board of Education* had made segregation illegal. Before this ruling black people and white people were often segregated. This means they were forced to go to separate institutions such as schools and restaurants.

President Eisenhower felt it was up to each state to decide how to end segregation in schools. Many southern states disregarded the Supreme Court's ruling. In September 1957, several black students attempted to attend Central High School in Little Rock, Arkansas, which is shown above. The Arkansas National Guard, an army troop called in by Arkansas governor Orval Faubus, blocked the black students from entering. Eisenhower ordered the Arkansas troops, as well as federal army troops, to keep order and oversee the integration. The children were allowed into the school.

1

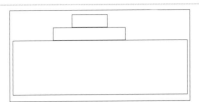

To begin drawing the Little Rock Central High School in Arkansas, draw a large rectangle. Inside this guide draw three smaller rectangular guides as shown. These guides will help you draw the shape of the building.

2

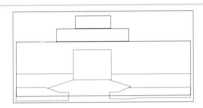

Draw a rectangle in the center of the bottom rectangle. Add a horizontal line on either side. Draw slanted lines from the bottom corners of the square. Draw two irregular shapes that extend from the slanted lines you just drew.

3

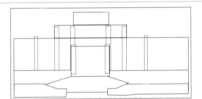

Erase the extra lines that go through the bottom shapes you made in step 2. Draw the vertical rectangles as shown. Notice that some rectangles are thinner and some are slightly thicker.

4

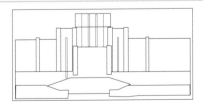

Erase any extra lines that cross inside the rectangles you made in the last step. Draw more vertical rectangles. The two in the front are especially thin. Add two vertical lines to the center section of the building.

5

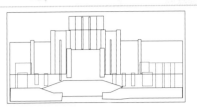

Add more rectangles and straight lines along the bottom of the building on the left side and on the right side. Add a horizontal line above the vertical lines and shapes on the right.

6

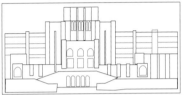

Erase any extra crossing lines inside the shapes you just made. Add rows of horizontal lines to make several floors of the building. Add windows and a column on the right. The windows have different widths. Some have curved tops. Some windows are rectangles.

7

Erase any extra lines. Add vertical lines to make the many classroom windows as shown. Add more horizontal lines for the windows. Take a moment to fix any windows or floors before you go on to the next step.

8

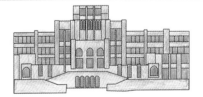

Erase the large rectangular guide you made in step 1. Finish your drawing of Central High School by shading. The windows and doors are darker than the other areas of the building.

The Arms Race

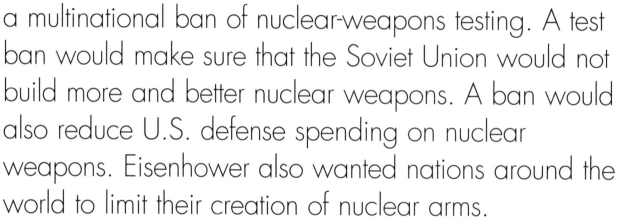

One of the most serious issues during President Eisenhower's second term was the advancement of nuclear arms. In 1958 and 1959, Eisenhower worked on a multinational ban of nuclear-weapons testing. A test ban would make sure that the Soviet Union would not build more and better nuclear weapons. A ban would also reduce U.S. defense spending on nuclear weapons. Eisenhower also wanted nations around the world to limit their creation of nuclear arms.

In May 1960, the Soviet Union leader Nikita Khrushchev refused to negotiate a ban on nuclear testing with the United States. Khrushchev is shown above to the right of Eisenhower. Khrushchev refused to negotiate after it was discovered that Eisenhower had approved U-2 spy planes to fly over the Soviet Union and take pictures. These images were to document the Soviet Union's nuclear activities. Eisenhower's best opportunity to slow the nuclear danger to the world had slipped away.

1

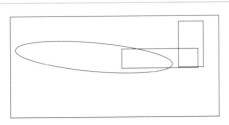

This cartoon shows President Eisenhower painting a dove on a U-2. The dove stands for peace. The cartoon is meant to represent Eisenhower's failure to create a test ban after the U-2 was shot down in the Soviet Union. To begin drawing the plane, make a rectangular guide. Next draw two small rectangles and an oval.

2

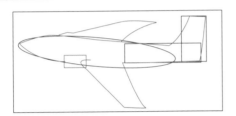

Use curving and straight lines to draw the two wings, the body, and the tail of the plane as shown. Use the shapes you made in step 1 to help you with this. Then add a small rectangular guide on the bottom of the plane.

3

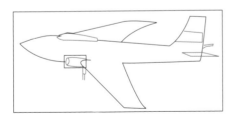

Erase the guides you made in step 1. Draw a curved shape inside the small rectangular guide you made in step 2. Then below this shape add a small shape and two lines as shown. Draw the curved shape along the top of the plane for the window. Add shapes to the plane's tail with slanted and straight lines.

4

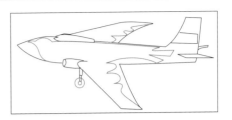

Erase the guide shape you made in step 2. Erase the extra lines that go through the tail of the plane. Next draw two small circles for the wheel. Draw the dove that decorates the plane using curving lines. In some areas you will use looping and wavy lines. Notice how the wings of the bird are placed over the wings of the plane.

5

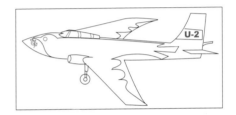

Write "U-2" along the tail of the plane as shown. Next draw a small circle for the eye of the dove. Then draw the leaves and branches that the dove holds in its beak. Add curving lines as shown for the window of the plane.

6

Erase the large rectangular guide you made in step 1. Finish your drawing of the U-2 by shading the plane. The areas that include the dove, the word "U-2," and parts of the window should remain white. Shade the other areas of your drawing dark.

Eisenhower's Legacy

Even as Dwight D. Eisenhower worked to protect America from the dangers of Communism and nuclear war, he also refused to spend too much money on missiles and nuclear arms. He made his farewell address to the nation in January 1961. In it President Eisenhower, a man who once led the army, warned against heavy defense spending.

As president, Eisenhower created the interstate highway system, which provided government funding for the construction of several federal highways across the United States. These highways allowed cars and trucks to travel the country quickly and easily.

After Eisenhower left the presidency, he and Mamie enjoyed a quiet life on their farm in Gettysburg, Pennsylvania. His son, John, and grandchildren lived nearby. In retirement Eisenhower wrote books about his time in the White House. In March 1969, he died at Walter Reed Army Hospital in Washington, D.C. Dwight D. Eisenhower had led the United States and its allies to victory in World War II and was president during a period of peace and growth for America.

1 To begin drawing Dwight D. Eisenhower draw a rectangular guide. Next draw an oval guide for the head. Draw two smaller ovals for the hands. Make guides for the body, shoulders, and arms.

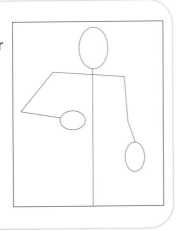

2 Draw horizontal and vertical lines as guides for the eyes, nose, and mouth. Add an oval guide for the back of the chair and a rectangle for the seat. Draw two small lines beneath the seat.

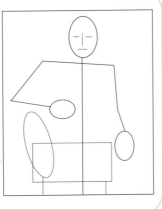

3 Add long ovals to flesh out your guides for Eisenhower's arms. Draw the body and legs of the chair as shown.

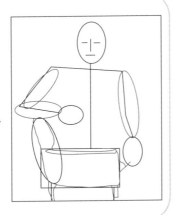

4 Erase the guides for the chair. Use lines to outline his head, shoulders, arms, and legs.

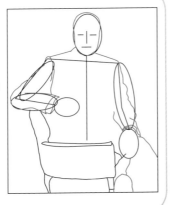

5 Erase the guides for the head, shoulders, and arms. Use squiggly and curving lines to draw his ears, hands, and fingers as shown. Add his hair. Use straight lines to draw the collar and the sides of his jacket.

6 Erase the vertical guide for the body and the oval guides for the hands. Add details to the eyes, nose, and mouth. Add curved lines for the shirt, tie, and vest, as shown.

7 Erase the guides for the eyes, nose, and mouth. Use curved lines for his glasses as shown. Add lines for the folds on his sleeves, vest, jacket, and leg. Add circles for vest buttons and for details on the chair.

8 Erase the rectangular guide you made in step 1. Finish your drawing of President Eisenhower by shading.

Timeline

1890 Dwight David Eisenhower is born on October 14, in Denison, Texas.

1892 The Eisenhower family moves to Abilene, Kansas.

1911 Eisenhower enters the United States Military Academy at West Point, in New York.

1914 World War I begins.

1915 Eisenhower graduates from West Point and becomes a second lieutenant serving in the U.S. Army in Texas.

1916 Mamie Geneva Doud and Dwight Eisenhower are married in Denver, Colorado.

1918 Eisenhower serves in the new Tank Corps, conducting tank training during World War I at Camp Colt, near Gettysburg, Pennsylvania. World War I ends.

1922–1924 Eisenhower serves as an officer to General Fox Conner in Panama.

1935–1939 Eisenhower serves as a military aide and adviser to General MacArthur in the Philippines.
World War II begins in 1939.

1940–1943 Eisenhower rises through the army ranks to be appointed supreme commander, or head, of the Allied Expeditionary Forces, in December 1943, during World War II.

1944 Eisenhower commands the forces of D-Day, the Normandy invasion, on June 6.

1945 Eisenhower becomes the chief of staff of the U.S. Army.

1948 Eisenhower accepts a position as the president of Columbia University in New York.

1950 Eisenhower is named the supreme allied commander of the army of the North Atlantic Treaty Organization (NATO).

1952 Eisenhower announces his candidacy for president. He is elected in November and takes office the following year.

1953 The Korean War ends.

1957 Eisenhower sends federal troops to Little Rock, Arkansas, to allow black students into the local high school. This was done to put into effect the Supreme Court decision in *Brown v. Board of Education*.

1960 A U-2 spy plane sent by the United States is shot down over the Soviet Union.

1961 The Eisenhowers move to Gettysburg, Pennsylvania.

1969 Eisenhower dies on March 28, 1969. He is buried in Abilene, Kansas.

Glossary

Allies (A-lyz) The countries that fought against the Axis powers in World War II. The Allies were Britain, Canada, China, France, the Soviet Union, and the United States.

civilian (sih-VIL-yin) A person who is not in the military.

civil rights (SIH-vul RYTS) The rights that citizens have.

Communist (KOM-yuh-nist) Belonging to a system in which all the land, houses, and factories belong to the government and are shared by everyone.

conservative (kun-SER-vuh-tiv) Favoring established views and values. Someone who is conservative tends to oppose change.

constitutional (kon-stuh-TOO-shnul) Having to do with the basic rules by which the United States is governed.

defeat (dih-FEET) A loss.

defended (dih-FEND-ed) Guarded.

institutions (in-stuh-TOO-shunz) Established organizations, such as schools or museums.

integration (in-tuh-GRAY-shun) The act of bringing together groups from different races, sexes, and social classes.

Korean War (kuh-REE-un WOR) A conflict that lasted from 1950 to 1953 between North Korea, aided by China, and South Korea, aided by United Nations forces, which consisted largely of U.S. troops.

Nazi (NOT-see) Having to do with the German political party led by Adolf Hitler during World War II.

nuclear (NOO-klee-ur) Having to do with the power created by splitting atoms, the smallest bits of matter.

Supreme Court (suh-PREEM KORT) The highest court in the United States.

World War I (WURLD WOR WUN) The war fought between the Allies and the Central powers from 1914 to 1918.

Index

Web Sites

Due to the changing nature of Internet links, PowerKids Press has developed an online list of Web sites related to the subject of this book. This site is updated regularly. Please use this link to access the list:
www.powerkidslinks.com/kgdpusa/eisenhower/